D1413030

INSIDE WOODY ALLEN

Inside Woody Allen

Selections from the Comic Strip

Drawn by Stuart Hample

CORONET BOOKS
Hodder and Stoughton

"Inside Woody Allen" is syndicated in newspapers throughout the United States. It also appears in over sixty foreign countries.

Copyright © 1978 by IWA Enterprises Inc.
Hackenbush Productions Inc.

First published in Great Britain 1978 by Robson Books Limited

Coronet edition 1979

This book is sold subject to the condition that it shall not, by way of trade or otherwise, be lent, re-sold, hired out or otherwise circulated without the publisher's prior consent in any form of binding or cover other than that in which this is published and without a similar condition including this condition being imposed on the subsequent purchaser.

Printed and bound in Great Britain for Hodder and Stoughton Paperbacks, a division of Hodder and Stoughton Ltd., Mill Road, Dunton Green, Sevenoaks, Kent (Editorial Office: 47 Bedford Square, London, WC1 3DP) by Fletcher & Son Ltd, Norwich

ISBN 0 340 24497 6

PHILOSOPHY

Private Journal - Entry #1.010
I was going to write my autobiography.

But then I remembered—

You should only write about things you know about.

THERE'S NO WAY YOU CAN PROVE THERE ISN'T A GOD.
RIGHT. YOU JUST HAVE TO TAKE IT ON FAITH.

JOHN STUART MILL SAYS THE GOOD IS THAT WHICH BRINGS THE GREATEST PLEASURE TO THE GREATEST NUMBER.
I SEE THAT. BUT WHAT IF THERE'S DISAGREEMENT OVER WHAT BRINGS PLEASURE?
IN THAT CASE YOU KILL ONE ANOTHER.

"MY WATCH BROKE, SO INSTEAD OF BUYING A NEW ONE, I DECIDED TO CALL UP THE TIME OPERATOR ON THE PHONE. WELL, THIS TURNED OUT TO BE A NOT ENTIRELY CONVENIENT METHOD. SO I SPENT A DAY LISTENING TO THE RECORDING, MAKING A TRANSCRIPT. NOW WHEN I WANT TO KNOW THE TIME, I CAN JUST LOOK IT UP."

Private Journal-Entry # 1,092
Some artists achieve immortality through their work.

I prefer to achieve mine through not dying.

IF THERE WERE A JUST GOD...

—THEN HE'D HAVE US EATING TWICE A WEEK AND MAKING LOVE THREE TIMES A DAY.

GOD IS SILENT.

NOW IF WE CAN ONLY GET MAN TO SHUT UP.

DR. HELMHOLTZ, ARE HUMANS IN A STATE OF NATURE SAVAGES— AS HOBBES THOUGHT— OR INNOCENT, LOVING CREATURES— AS ROUSSEAU THOUGHT?
IT DEPENDS.
WEEKDAYS, HOBBES WAS RIGHT. WEEKENDS, ROUSSEAU.

"WOODS," DO YOU BELIEVE MIND AND BODY ARE ONE?
UM...

I GUESS I THINK SO **NOW**...

BUT TRY ASKING ME IN BED.

Private Journal - Entry #3,071
300 years after Descartes' death, his fundamental insight remains valid.

But unfortunately, now it reads, "I thought, therefore I was."

I ALWAYS WONDER HOW THEY GET ALL THOSE CLOWNS INTO ONE LITTLE CAR.
THAT'S THE DIFFERENCE BETWEEN US...
I ALWAYS WONDER WHY.

YOU'RE LATE AGAIN!
LISTEN, I JUST CAME FROM TEACHING A PHILOSOPHY CLASS, AND WE PROVED THERE IS NO SUCH THING AS TIME.
WHAT HAPPENED NOW, HAPPENED BEFORE, WILL HAPPEN AGAIN, HAS ALWAYS HAPPENED, IS HAPPENING, AND WILL ALWAYS HAPPEN.
YEAH, BUT WHAT IF YOU'RE 45 MINUTES LATE?

GEE, I'VE BEEN WAITING A LONG TIME...
DR. FOBICK
FWW
... I'M ALREADY UP TO THE 1957 ISSUES OF "FOOTWEAR WEEKLY."
DR. FOBICK
FWW
WHEN THE MIND HAS NO OBJECT BUT TIME, TIME SLOWS DOWN.
DR. FOBICK
New
FWW

I WONDER IF THAT'S TRUE OF SPACE ALSO.
THE IMPORTANT THING IS TO HAVE SOMETHING TO OCCUPY MY MIND.
DR. FOBICK
HM, IS IT TRUE OF SPACE ALSO?
DR. FOBICK
SPACE! DISTANCE!
ROOM...
POP!
WELL, I GUESS I'LL NEVER KNOW. WONDER WHAT TIME IT IS.
DR. FOBICK

A WORLD WITHOUT POLLUTION, WITHOUT CRIME, HUNGER, POVERTY!

CAN YOU EVEN IMAGINE IT?
SURE, I'M THINKING OF ONE NOW

URANUS.

THE TROUBLE WITH POSTERITY IS, BY THE TIME YOU HAVE IT, IT'S TOO LATE TO USE FOR AN "I TOLD-YOU-SO."

Private Journal - Entry 3,774
Man is a creature doomed to exist in "Time...".

- even though that is not where the action is.

IN PHILOSOPHY, A GOOD QUESTION IS MORE IMPORTANT THAN A GOOD ANSWER.
WHAT'S A GOOD QUESTION?

THAT IS.
WHAT'S THE ANSWER?

THIS IS.

DO YOU BELIEVE IN GOD?
I'M NOT SURE.
WELL, KIERKEGAARD SAYS IF YOU'RE NOT SURE, YOU DON'T.
OK, THEN I GUESS I DO.

PSYCHIATRY

SINCE THIS IS YOUR FIRST DAY OF ANALYSIS, ALLOW ME TO READ THIS CARD BEFORE WE BEGIN-

"YOU HAVE THE RIGHT TO REMAIN SILENT.

"ANYTHING YOU SAY MAY BE USED AGAINST YOU."

342

I'M MR. ALLEN – FOR DR. FOBICK...

ER... MR. ALLEN, DR. FOBICK SAID TO TELL YOU SHE'LL BE RIGHT BACK...
THANKS.

WHILE YOU'RE WAITING, I JUST WANT TO SAY THAT YOU'VE GIVEN ME MANY HOURS OF JOY.
OH, YOU'RE A FAN OF MINE, HUH?

I'LL SAY! I NEVER MISS A SESSION.
342
WHAT?

WHEN YOU GO UP AND TALK TO THE DOCTOR ABOUT YOUR PRIVATE LIFE, I LEAVE THE INTERCOM ON.
OH?

I TELL YOU, EVERY DOORMAN ON THE BLOCK COMES TO LISTEN...

YOU'RE VERY POPULAR AROUND HERE.
GEE, I HAD NO IDEA I HAD AN AUDIENCE OUT THERE...

...I GUESS THOSE TV RATINGS WERE WRONG AFTER ALL....

WOODY, DO YOU EVER GET DEJA VU? YOU KNOW, THE FEELING THAT EVERYTHING YOU DO HAS HAPPENED BEFORE?
NEVER.
WOODY, DO YOU EVER GET DEJA VU? YOU KNOW, THE FEELING THAT EVERYTHING YOU DO HAS HAPPENED BEFORE?
NEVER.
SAY, WOODY...
UH, PUT ME DOWN FOR A "YES," WILL YOU?

DR. HELMHOLTZ, DO YOU BELIEVE THAT PSYCHOLOGISTS HAVE AN OVER-FONDNESS FOR LABELING EMOTIONAL OR INTELLECTUAL STATES?
NO, OF COURSE NOT.

OH, BY THE WAY, YOU ARE REFERRING TO WHAT WE TERM "NOMANDATUS."

...SO, YOU SEE, YOU ARE A UNIQUE INDIVIDUAL. NOW GO OUT AND BE YOURSELF.

FOR A WHILE THERE. I WAS ACTUALLY HAVING AN IDENTITY CRISIS...

"I DO NOT LIKE DEALING WITH ELECTRICAL APPLIANCES...

"...BECAUSE THEY ARE GENERALLY HOSTILE.

"MY TOASTER GAVE ME PROBLEMS FROM THE INSTANT I BOUGHT IT.
POW!

"SO I HAD TO LET IT KNOW THAT I WAS ITS MASTER...

"... I TOOK A FORK AND TRIED TO MAKE A FEW MINOR ADJUSTMENTS...

ZAP

"... AND A STRANGE THING HAPPENED.

"AFTER THE SHOCK– FOR THE FIRST TIME IN WEEKS I WASN'T DEPRESSED.

"NOW I DO IT WHEN I'M FEELING LOW."

I JUST GOT BACK FROM ENTERTAINING A PSYCHOANALYTIC CONVENTION IN VIENNA.
THE TOWN WAS CRAWLING WITH ANALYSTS. YOU COULD TELL THEY WERE ANALYSTS BECAUSE WHEN THEY GOT DRUNK...
Freud Born Here
CHARTER
479
...THEY KEPT SINGING "I WANT A GIRL, JUST LIKE THE GIRL WHO MARRIED DEAR OLD DAD..."

WHAT COMES TO MIND?
I KEEP HAVING THIS FANTASY THAT I AM A TWO-DIMENSIONAL CARTOON CHARACTER WHOSE DESTINY IS RULED BY AN UNSEEN ARTIST.

I THINK YOU'RE REALLY GOING OFF THE DEEP END NOW...

I REALIZE IT'S JUST TRANSFERENCE, DOCTOR FOBICK, BUT THESE DAYS, I'M MADLY IN LOVE WITH YOU.
"JUST TRANSFERENCE!" WITH THESE LEGS, HE THINKS IT'S "JUST TRANSFERENCE"?

DR. FOBICK, IS IT POSSIBLE TO DREAM ABSURD PUNS IN ONE'S SLEEP?
WHAT WAS THE DREAM?
I DREAMED I WAS IN A MATERNITY WARD AND ACTUALLY WITNESSED THE BIRTH OF THE BLUES.
IT'S TOO BAD I DON'T GET TO GRADE THESE SESSIONS ON A SCALE OF ONE-TO-TEN...

"MY SHRINK, DOCTOR FOBICK, HAS GONE ON VACATION FOR A MONTH...

"...AND AS THE DAYS WEAR ON, I FIND MYSELF CONFIDING MORE AND MORE IN OTHER PEOPLE..."
R. Gluck D.D.S.

SO, DOCTOR GLUCK, I'VE BEEN SEEING THIS NEW GIRL...
HEAD BACK, PLEASE.

...I THINK SHE LIKES ME A LOT...
OPEN, PLEASE.

...I CERTAINLY LIKE HER. I KNOW WE'RE FROM DIFFERENT BACKGROUNDS, BUT...
HMM... CAVITY...

BLUCHUGHNAAM...
RINSE.

SO ANYHOW, I FEEL I'M GOING TO GIVE THE RELATIONSHIP MY BEST TRY...
OPEN.

I LIKE DOCTOR GLUCK... HE'S SO UNDERSTANDING...

Private Journal - Entry 2,965:
Politics is the art of the possible.

Psychoanalysis, the art of the impossible.

I HAVE A LOVELY HOUSE IN THE SUBURBS, TWO WONDERFUL, HEALTHY CHILDREN...
A CHARMING, SUCCESSFUL HUSBAND, ALL MY MATERIAL NEEDS SATISFIED.
I HAVE ONLY ONE QUESTION...
IS THERE A WAY OUT?

THIS LAURA PERSON SOUNDS LIKE A WONDERFUL GIRL FOR YOU.
IN SOME WAYS. BUT SHE HAS FATAL FLAWS.

EVERY WOMAN HAS FLAWS. YOU MUST ACCEPT THEM.
I DO - SHE'S NEUROTIC AND COMPULSIVE AND HYSTERICAL ...

- BUT IT'S NOT ENOUGH FOR ME ...

WHEN DID YOU FIRST REALIZE YOUR MARRIAGE WAS IN TROUBLE?
WHEN THE EX-MRS. ALLEN BOUGHT AN ELECTRIC BLANKET...

AND BEFORE WE WENT TO BED...

...SHE TRIED TO SHAVE MY HEAD AND SLIT MY PAJAMA SLEEVES AND LEGS.

RELATIONS WITH WOMEN

Private Journal, Entry #2,377
There are only two things in life that are important.

One is sex.

And the other's not that important.

YOU'RE THE HANDSOMEST, WITTIEST, SEXIEST MAN I'VE EVER MET.
THIS GIRL IS FANTASTIC!

BUT CAN I TRUST HER JUDGMENT?

THE EX-MRS. ALLEN USED TO TELL ME I WAS IMMATURE AND ACTED LIKE A CHILD.
FINALLY, I GOT UP THE COURAGE TO CONFRONT THE ISSUE HEAD-ON.
FOR ONE ENTIRE DAY I PRACTICED WHAT I WOULD SAY TO HER...
...BUT WHEN SHE CAME HOME AND I RAISED MY HAND—SHE WOULDN'T CALL ON ME.

SHE'S EVERYTHING I COULD ASK FOR IN A WOMAN...
SO NOW I'M SPENDING HOURS RACKING MY BRAIN, TRYING TO THINK OF MORE THAT I COULD ASK FOR.

...AND THIS IS MY BEDROOM. AH, YES, IF THESE WALLS COULD ONLY TALK...

WE CAN TALK...
AND TAKE IT FROM US, NOTHING INTERESTING EVER HAPPENS.

"I AM NOT THE DEBONAIR SEX BANDIT I MAY APPEAR TO BE.

"THAT'S MERELY AN IMAGE I PROJECT. IN REALITY...

"I'M LONELY A LOT. BUT I'M NOT GOOD AT MEETING GIRLS...

"...I'VE USED ALL APPROACHES, SUCH AS THE MONTGOMERY CLIFT- STANDING- BROODING- PENSIVE- APPROACH.
I'M AT A PARTY... EVERYONE'S HAVING FUN.

"I'M OFF ALONE- PONDERING THE FATE OF MANKIND IN AN INDIFFERENT UNIVERSE NOT OF ITS OWN MAKING...

"NO ONE COMES NEAR ME- BUT I'M COOL...
LIFE IS VERY DEEP...
"BY 2 A.M. ALL THE OTHER GUESTS HAVE LEFT.
I WISH I COULD COME TO TERMS WITH MY IDENTITY.

"THE HOST AND HOSTESS EMPTY THE ASHTRAYS.
THANK HEAVEN IT'S OVER! I'M EXHAUSTED!
THEY STAYED SO LATE!
I'VE GOT TO GET THE RIGHT LEVEL OF ANGUISH.

WHEN YOU'RE THROUGH BROODING INTELLECTUALLY. WOULD YOU PUT OUT THE LIGHTS...
OH, GOD...
...AND GO HOME?

THE TROUBLE WITH MY SEX LIFE IS, TOO OFTEN IT TAKES PLACE WITH JUST ONE CONSENTING ADULT.

I USED TO VISIT THE MUSEUM A LOT BECAUSE IT OFFERED CULTURE, AND A CHANCE TO MEET FANTASTIC GIRLS...

I HAD MANY SERIOUS LOVE AFFAIRS WITH WOMEN I MET IN THE MUSEUM...

MUSEUM OF MO
ART ENDURES...

AN OLD GIRL OF MINE.

I DON'T KNOW IF IT WAS MY FAULT OR HERS, BUT WE HAD A TERRIBLY FALSE RELATIONSHIP.

IT FINALLY DAWNED ON ME WHEN I REALIZED EVERY TIME SHE HAD AN ORGASM, HER NOSE GREW LONGER.

MY ONE REGRET IN LIFE— ASIDE FROM THE FACT THAT I AM NOT WARREN BEATTY- IS THAT I'M NOT AN AMOEBA.
"AN AMOEBA JUST SPLITS AND FALLS IN LOVE WITH THE OTHER AMOEBA.
"THEN THEY SPLIT AND FALL IN LOVE AND SO ON, AD INFINITUM.
"MAYBE IF I JUST SPLIT..."
YOU NEVER TAKE ME ANYPLACE!
WE NEVER DO ANYTHING INTERESTING!
ALL YOU EVER DO IS BROOD! I THOUGHT YOU'D BE FUNNY!!
POP!
I THINK I'LL JUST GO BACK TO REGRETTING I'M NOT WARREN BEATTY.

Private Journal - Entry # 3,174.
Why do all the women in my life say I'm a lousy lover?

How can they make a definitive judgment in only 3 minutes?

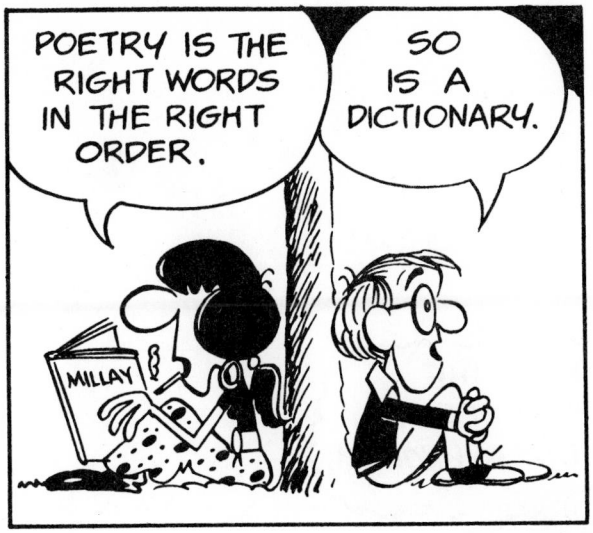
POETRY IS THE RIGHT WORDS IN THE RIGHT ORDER.
SO IS A DICTIONARY.
MILLAY

YES, BUT IF YOU WERE ALONE WITH A BEAUTIFUL WOMAN, WOULD YOU READ HER A DICTIONARY?

NOT UNLESS SHE DIDN'T UNDERSTAND THE MEANING OF THE WORD "FELLATIO."
MILLAY

IT'S HARD TO MEET GIRLS.
ONCE I TRIED THE "DOUBLE-REVERSE-DAVID NIVEN" APPROACH.
I AFFECTED A LITTLE MUSTACHE, SPOKE BRITISH, AND ACTED FATHERLY...
...AND I PICKED UP A GIRL WHO HAD A LITTLE MUSTACHE, SPOKE BRITISH, AND ACTED FATHERLY.

WELL, MAX, I ACTUALLY MET THAT PERFECT WOMAN WE SAW THE OTHER DAY.
AND SHE'S TOO PERFECT TO LIKE YOU, RIGHT? JUST LIKE ALL THE OTHERS.

NOT AT ALL. WE HAVE A DATE ON SATURDAY. OF COURSE I HAD TO LIE FEROCIOUSLY.
YOU'LL NEVER LEARN! SHE'LL DUMP YOU ONCE SHE FINDS OUT THE TRUTH...

BUT SHE **WON'T** FIND OUT THE TRUTH...AS LONG AS I CAN FIND A WAY TO GET FREE RUN OF BUCKINGHAM PALACE ON SATURDAY NIGHT.

HELLO, I'M NOT HOME... PLEASE LEAVE YOUR MESSAGE WHEN YOU HEAR THE BEEP...

JUST WHAT I NEED, ANOTHER GIRL WITH AN ANSWERING MACHINE. IT'S SO COLD AND IMPERSONAL

THE HUMAN ELEMENT IS GONE. NO EMOTIONS, NO FEELINGS...

...HEY — SHE SOUNDS GREAT FOR ME!

4

FAMILY HISTORY & EARLY CHILDHOOD

OH! HOW CUTE! OUR WOODY'S BRONZED BABY SHOES.
THEY DO BRING BACK MEMORIES...

YES, HIS TINY LITTLE HANDS TRYING TO FILE HIS FEET FREE.

"I PUT IN 12 YEARS OF RESEARCH AT THE NATIONAL LIBRARY OF INDIAN AFFAIRS...
VOL 4
THE ALLENS IN AMERICA

"...TO UNEARTH THIS HAIR-RAISING STORY FROM THE ALLEN FAMILY HISTORY.
VOL 4
THE ALLENS IN

"WHEN MY GRANDFATHER WAS A BOY, HE WAS KIDNAPPED BY INDIANS FROM THE ALLEN FAMILY HOMESTEAD IN YUMA.
"THE INDIANS RAISED HIM WITH LOVE...
IF YOU LISTEN AFTER 6, THE RATES ARE CHEAPER.
"...BUT IT WAS DIFFICULT BEING THE ONLY ONE IN THE TRIBE WITH RED HAIR AND GLASSES.

HEY, CAN I GO BUFFALO HUNTING WITH YOU GUYS?
YOU, "FOUR-EYES"? HA! HA!
"BUT WHEN MY GREAT-GRANDFATHER LED THE ALLEN CLAN TO RESCUE HIS SON, IT WAS A DISASTER BECAUSE...

"...WHEN INDIANS ATTACK, WAGONS ARE SUPPOSED TO FORM A CIRCLE, LIKE AN "O", BUT HE DIDN'T KNOW THE ALPHABET...

"SO INSTEAD OF AN "O", HE HAD THEM FORM THE LETTER "G"...
"AND THE INDIANS CAME IN THE OPENING AND MASSACRED THEM!"

"I THINK MY PARENTS WOULD HAVE BEEN PERFECTLY HAPPY IF I HAD BECOME A PHARMACIST...
ALLEN'S DISCOUNT DRUGS
Sale
"OR A SUCCESSFUL DIAMOND SALESMAN.
$500
"BUT I HAD MY OWN DREAM...
"FROM THE TIME I WAS A KID, I ALWAYS WANTED TO BE AN ACTOR, BUT I WAS TOO SHY TO SPEAK UP...
TO BE OR NOT TO BE...
LOUDER!
WHAT?
"THEN I READ THAT DEMOSTHENES, THE GREAT GREEK ORATOR, ALSO SPOKE UNCLEARLY WHEN HE WAS YOUNG...
ἶναι ἢ οὐκ ἶναι...
Τί?
"AND HE CURED HIMSELF BY SPEAKING WITH PEBBLES IN HIS MOUTH.
"SO I TRIED IT...
1
2
"...AND I LEARNED TO SPEAK LOUD...
POO BE, OR MOP POO BE...
"...BUT I BECAME DEPENDENT ON THE PEBBLES, AND COULD ONLY TALK WHEN THEY WERE IN MY MOUTH.
I MUV YOU...
WHA-AT?
"THAT WAS O.K. UNTIL I APPEARED IN A SCHOOL PLAY DURING HAY-FEVER SEASON.
AHH... AHH...
"I SNEEZED IN THE FIRST ACT...
CHOO
"...AND GAVE MR. POE, THE PRINCIPAL, A FRACTURED SKULL."

"SCENES FROM MY CHILD-HOOD."
OUR SON MAY NOT BE HANDSOME, SOPHIE, BUT AT LEAST HE'S MUSICAL.
HE ONLY MISSES BEING A BEAUTIFUL CHILD BY AN INCH.
TRUE. HE MISSES BY AN INCH...
...BUT KEEPS GOING...
AND WINDS UP 4,000 MILES FROM IT.

"I GUESS I WAS NEVER QUITE LIKE OTHER KIDS..."
HEY, DUKE, KNOCK THE DODGERS FOR A LOOP!
CAN I HAVE YOUR AUTOGRAPH, DUKE?
LEMME TAKE YOUR PICTURE, DUKE!
DUKE, DO YOU THINK THERE'S SUCH A THING AS FREE WILL?

"IF YOU'RE A POOR KID IN THE CITY, YOU SELDOM SEE GRASS OR TREES.
"I GUESS THAT'S WHY THE SUBURBS ARE EVERYONE'S DREAM."
IT'S CHILLY IN HERE, HOWARD.
I'LL TURN ON THE FIRE.
CLICK
SETH! JENNIFER! WE'RE GOING TO SIT AROUND THE COZY FIRE WITH UNCLE WOODY.
C'MON, FRAMPTON.

THAT'S NOT A FIRE, IT'S JUST A LIGHT BULB!
WANNA ROAST MARSHMALLOWS, KIDS?
NEAT-O!
ROAST MARSHMALLOWS, OVER A FAKE FIRE?
IT'S OK, WE USE PREROASTED ONES.
I'LL PUT ON ANOTHER LOG...
THE SUBURBS ARE EVERYONE'S DREAM...
...MAYBE THAT'S WHY THEY SEEM SO UNREAL.

MY PARENTS HAD TROUBLE APPROACHING THINGS CORRECTY.
FOR INSTANCE WHEN SUSPECTED I HAD A TENDENCY TOWARD MASOCHISM...
...THEY TRIED TO BEAT IT OUT OF ME.

MY PARENTS ARE DEVIOUS. THEY TOLD ME I OWED MY PHYSICAL EXISTENCE TO THEM...
...BUT I, ALONE, AM RESPONSIBLE FOR MY SPIRITUAL EXISTENCE.
DEVIOUS? THAT'S VERY PROFOUND.
MAYBE. BUT THEY USED IT TO PERSUADE ME TO PAY THEM RENT ON MY BODY TILL I WAS 21.

ALLEN FAMILY HISTORY

I PAID FIFTY DOLLARS TO GET THIS STORY FROM MY GENEALOGY...

"BACK IN THE FIFTH CENTURY, THE HUNS, THE MOST VICIOUS, CRUEL BARBARIANS IN HISTORY, WERE GOING TO INVADE A TOWN...

"...AND THE TOWN CALLED FOR VOLUNTEERS...

THEY NEEDED WARRIORS, AND THE ALLEN CLAN, WHICH BY THEN WAS VERY LARGE, THOUGHT THEY SAID "FURRIERS."
ALLEN FAMILY HISTORY

"AND MY FAMILY, WHICH WAS ALWAYS IN THE GARMENT BUSINESS, UNKNOWINGLY MARCHED OUT ARMED WITH NOTHING BUT NEEDLES AND THREAD AND TAPE MEASURES...

"...AND THEY CONFRONTED THE HUGE HUN ARMY...
?

"...AND ATTILA, THE HUN LEADER, WAS SO MOVED BY THEIR NAIVE BRAVERY...

HE SLAUGHTERED THEM ON THE SPOT!
ALLEN FAMILY HISTORY

MY PARENTS REALLY DIDN'T UNDERSTAND CHILDREN.
HOW SO ?

BEFORE I WAS BORN, MY MOTHER WENT TO SEE A PSYCHIATRIST.

SHE COMPLAINED I WAS CONSTANTLY SLEEPING IN A FETAL POSITION.

ARTIST/CELEBRITY

HEY! WOODY ALLEN! I WANT TO THANK YOU FOR GIVING ME LOTS OF LAUGHS!
YOU SEE MY MOVIES?
NO, I HAVE THE WINDOW OPPOSITE YOUR BEDROOM.

CAN I HAVE SOME EXTRA TICKETS FOR MY PERFORMANCE TONIGHT?
SOME FRIENDS ARE COMING INTO TOWN.
WOODY ALLEN Dec.4
BOX OFFICE
TONITE IN PERSON
SORRY IT'S ON SUCH SHORT NOTICE.
NO PROBLEM, MR. ALLEN. HERE'S 400.
YOU DON'T HAPPEN TO HAVE A BIG FAMILY, DO YOU? SAY ABOUT 2,500?

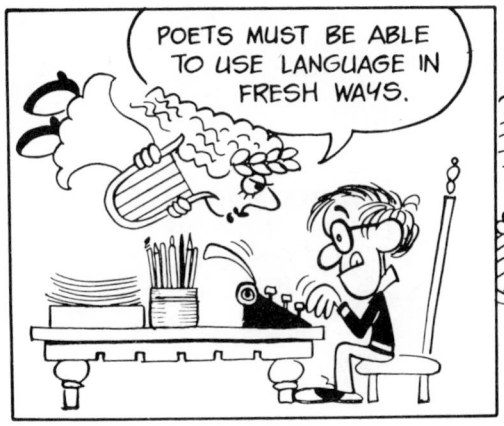
POETS MUST BE ABLE TO USE LANGUAGE IN FRESH WAYS.

THEY MUST ABJURE CLICHES.
THAT'S ME IN A NUTSHELL.

YOU COULDN'T HAVE RESISTED?

HMM-IF THEY'VE REALLY TRAINED DOLPHINS TO TALK...
Scientific American

HELLO, I'M WOODY ALLEN...
YOU THE GUY WHO MAKES THE FUNNY MOVIES?

"I MEET A TALKING DOLPHIN WHO IS QUITE ARTICULATE. WE START HAVING A DISCUSSION."
DO YOU LIKE INGMAR BERGMAN'S FILMS?
I LIKE PLANKTON...
THE CONSTANT, UNRELIEVED GLOOM, THE INTENSITY OF FEELING...
WHAT DO YOU THINK ABOUT SQUID?

...THE RELIGIOUS SOLEMNITY... IT'S HYPNOTIC.
I'M GETTING INTO ALGAE.

I ADMIRE THE STARKNESS OF HIS OVERALL VISION...

YOU EVER EAT ANY SEAWEED?

IT'S INTERESTING TO TALK TO A DOLPHIN, BUT YOU CAN NEVER GET INTO ANY SERIOUS ISSUES...
GEE, SHOW-BUSINESS PEOPLE ARE REALLY BORING...

TELL THE LIGHTING MAN TO CUT THE OVERHEADS. THEY EMPHASIZE MY NOSE.

THE SPOTLIGHTS MAKE MY GLASSES GLEAM. KILL 'EM.

GOOD, BUT THE WING LIGHTS MAKE ME LOOK SKINNY.

PERFECT. NOW I FEEL I LOOK MY BEST.

I'VE HAD BAD EXPERIENCES HOSTING TELETHONS...

"THE FIRST TIME I DID ONE...
HE'S SO SHORT...

"I HOSTED AN OFFBEAT TELETHON
WE HAD 24 HOURS TO RAISE 2 MILLION DOLLARS.
HELP NEUROTICS PAY FOR THEIR ANALYTIC SESSIONS.

"THE PHONES WERE ANSWERED BY 25 DEPRESSED COFFEE-HOUSE WAITRESSES WHO WANTED TO BE ACTRESSES
I WANT TO DONATE $25
I'M SORRY, SIR, I'M NOT READY TO RECEIVE YET

THIS MAN IS AFRAID TO SLEEP IN THE DARK.
9 YEARS AND $20,000 FOR PSYCHOTHERAPY WITH NO PROGRESS.

PLEASE GIVE GENEROUSLY TO HELP KEEP A LIGHT ON IN THIS MAN'S ROOM...
PSST-I ALSO NEED A RUBBER SHEET.

HERE'S A $200 PLEDGE FROM THE LATENT PARANOIDS DOWN AT AL'S DELI IN TENAFLY, NEW JERSEY.
1st Annual Neurotic Telethon
"THE FIRST 5 MINUTES WERE GREAT UNTIL A GROUP OF DRUNK TEXAS OIL MEN PHONED IN AND PLEDGED THE ENTIRE AMOUNT...

W-WE'RE OVER THE TOP...
"AND I STILL HAD 23 HOURS AND 55 MINUTES OF AIR TIME TO FILL..."

DON'T WORRY, WOODY, IT WAS JUST A BAD AUDIENCE.

SNEAK PREVIEW TONITE
WOODY ALLEN FILM

HEY, WOODY! I SEEN ALL YOUR MOVIES!
THANK YOU.
IT'S TOO BAD YOUR SENSE OF WHAT'S FUNNY IS SO OBVIOUS, YOUR IMPLICATIONS SO NARROW, AND YOUR COMIC PERSONA SO LACKING IN GENUINE INSPIRATION.
NOW I UNDERSTAND WHAT PEOPLE HAVE AGAINST HARD HATS

AREN'T YOU WOODY ALLEN?
YES.
SAY SOME-THING FUNNY.
WELL, I DON'T DO ROUTINES IN THE STREET...
THAT'S NOT FUNNY.
WELL, WOULD YOU SETTLE FOR AN AUTOGRAPH?
THAT'S NOT FUNNY.
WELL...
FORGET IT.

"MY PARENTS WANTED ME TO BE A PHARMACIST INSTEAD OF A WRITER...
Sale
ALLEN'S CUT-RATE DR

"AND SOMETIMES I THINK MAYBE I SHOULD HAVE LISTENED TO THEM.

"WHEN 'PLAY IT AGAIN, SAM' WAS TRYING OUT IN PHILADELPHIA, THE THIRD ACT WASN'T GETTING ENOUGH LAUGHS.
HERE'S LOOKIN' AT YOU, KID.

"I'M UP ONE NIGHT REWRITING SCENES WHEN THE DEVIL APPEARS.
I'LL FIX THE LAST ACT IN RETURN FOR YOUR SOUL.

WHAT ELSE HAVE YOU DONE?
I WORKED WITH ABE BURROWS ON "CACTUS FLOWER."

"WE SIGN THE DEAL. I SPLIT FOR MIAMI. I GET A CALL FROM PHILADELPHIA. THE DEVIL IS IN TROUBLE.

"I FLY UP IMMEDIATELY.
THE PLOT IS WEAK! THE CHARACTERIZATIONS ARE FLIMSY!

"WE HAVE A FIGHT AND SUE EACH OTHER.
ARGGH!
"HE SELLS MY SOUL TO A SYNDICATE THAT OWNS HOTELS IN LAS VEGAS AND HE GETS OUT WITH CASH."

YOU'D LIKE TO WRITE A SERIOUS NOVEL, RIGHT?
YES.
I HAVE A SURE-FIRE IDEA, WHICH I'LL DICTATE TO YOU.
OKAY, GO AHEAD.
"CALL ME ISHMAEL..."
TAP TAP
SOMETHING TELLS ME THIS WILL HAVE A HUGE PRE-SOLD PUBLIC.

YOU'RE WOODY ALLEN!
YES. I'D LIKE A HOT FUDGE SUNDAE BUT NO WHIPPED CREAM.
YOU'RE WOODY ALLEN...
ER- THE SUNDAE?
Y-YOU'RE WOODY ALLEN!
HOT FUDGE MAKES ME BREAK OUT, ANYWAY.
...AND HE DIDN'T EVEN LEAVE A TIP...

FORCES OF EVIL

7
5
3
L
L

FOR THIS E.S.P. EXPERIMENT TO WORK, YOU HAVE TO KEEP YOUR MIND BLANK.
O.K., I'M THINKING ABOUT LAST NIGHT.
I'M THINKING OF A COMMON HOUSEHOLD OBJECT. DO YOU READ ME?
MAYBE. ARE YOU THINKING OF MY STEREO?
NO. I WAS FOCUSING ON AN ENCHANTED MONKEY'S PAW.
NOT EVERY HOUSEHOLD HAS ONE OF THOSE.
REALLY? THEN HOW DO THEY SUMMON THE DEAD?

FOR THOSE WHO ENJOY A TALE OF THE BIZARRE...
Science and Sanity

...HERE'S ANOTHER IN A SERIES OF UNEXPLAINABLE PHENOMENA.
Science and Sanity

I REMEMBER MY ONE EXPERIENCE WITH THE OCCULT.
Science and Sanity
"EVERY NIGHT AT MIDNIGHT, THE GHOST OF A 1926 PACKARD WOULD DRIVE THROUGH MY LIVING ROOM...

"I CALLED THE BUREAU OF PSYCHIC RESEARCH
THEY SAID:
...NEXT TIME IT DRIVES THROUGH, GET THE LICENSE NUMBER.

"THE PACKARD APPEARED AGAIN THE FOLLOWING MIDNIGHT...

AH, I GOT THE NUMBER.
"I CALLED THE BUREAU AND GAVE THEM THE LICENSE NUMBER."
I'M SORRY, SIR, THERE'S NOTHING WE CAN DO... IT'S A RENTED CAR...

"WHEN I'M DRIVING, I MAKE IT A PRACTICE NEVER TO STOP LATE AT NIGHT FOR HITCH-HIKERS.

"BUT SOMETIMES DETERMINATION IS NOT ENOUGH...

"ARMED ONLY WITH A SPORTS CAR AND MY FATAL GOOD LOOKS, I SPEED ALONG A SECLUDED ROAD AT NIGHT...

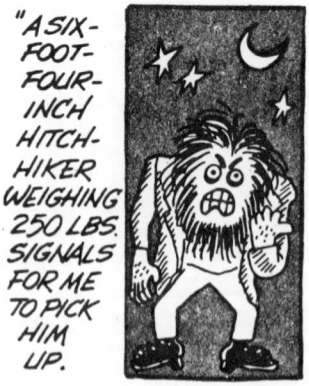
"A SIX-FOOT-FOUR-INCH HITCH-HIKER WEIGHING 250 LBS. SIGNALS FOR ME TO PICK HIM UP.

"SHREWDLY, I PASS HIM AT 70 M.P.H.
"HE GETS IN."

TURN ON THE RADIO, "FOUR-EYES."
YOU BET, SIR!
"WE INTERRUPT THIS PROGRAM TO BRING YOU A SPECIAL BULLETIN... THERE IS AN ESCAPED MANIAC AT LARGE...

"ALL VICTIMS, SO FAR, ARE SHORT RED-HEADED MEN WEARING GLASSES."
WHEW! THANK HEAVEN HE SAID "SHORT."

WHERE YOU GOIN', "RED"?
BROOKLYN.

GOOD. YOU CAN DROP ME.
WHERE?

CHICAGO.
WHAT THE HECK, IT'S ON MY WAY...

"I THREW THE I CHING...

"... AND GOT THE HEXAGRAM:

"'SHOVE OFF, JEWBOY.'"

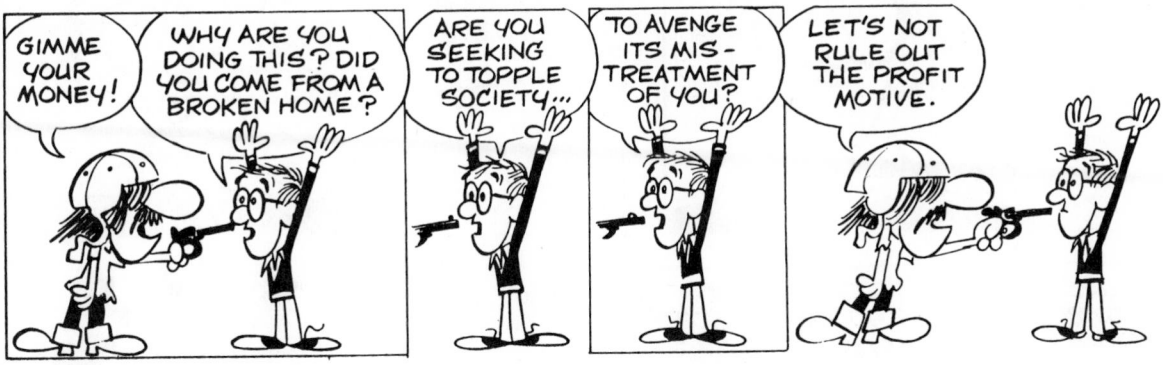
GIMME YOUR MONEY!
WHY ARE YOU DOING THIS? DID YOU COME FROM A BROKEN HOME?
ARE YOU SEEKING TO TOPPLE SOCIETY...
TO AVENGE ITS MIS-TREATMENT OF YOU?
LET'S NOT RULE OUT THE PROFIT MOTIVE.

AGAIN
AGAIN
NOW THAT'S WHAT I CALL A REAL CULT MOVIE.

SPICY FOODS GIVE ME HEARTBURN AND NIGHTMARES.

FOR EXAMPLE: LAST NIGHT, AFTER EATING A PASTRAMI, ONION AND CORNED BEEF ON RYE...

"I DREAM I SAVE A TOWN FROM DESTRUCTION BY A HORDE OF FIERCE VAMPIRE BATS IN METS' UNIFORMS.

"BUT AS THE TOWNFOLK CONGRATULATE ME, THE BATS BEGIN FLYING AROUND.

"I'M TERRIFIED THAT THEY'LL LAND ON ME AND TEAR ME APART.

"BUT SUDDENLY I REALIZE THAT I'M STANDING ON THE RUNWAY OF JFK AIRPORT...

"I BREAK INTO A RUN, GRAB A CAB, AND MAKE MY ESCAPE...

"WHILE THE AIR TRAFFIC CONTROLLER KEEPS THE BATS STACKED OVER THE AIRPORT FOR ANOTHER TWO HOURS..."

I WAS ONCE QUIZZED BY THE F.B.I. ON MY LOYALTY.

THEY WANTED TO KNOW WHAT I THOUGHT ABOUT ADOLPH EICHMANN.

I DIDN'T KNOW WHICH ANSWER WOULD SATISFY THEM.

CRIMINALS ARE SICK, AND DESERVE OUR SYMPATHY...

...AS LONG AS THEY'RE ATTACKING SOMEONE ELSE.

"I WAS VISITING MY SISTER MURIEL WHEN A THIEF BROKE INTO HER HOUSE."
HERE? IN THE SUBURBS? I THOUGHT THIS HAPPENED ONLY IN THE CITY.
I COMMUTE.
GIMME YOUR VALUABLES.

YES! SETH'S FIRST TOOTH. JENNY'S ART PRIZE FROM CAMP.
ARE YOU BEING FUNNY?
NO, IT'S JUST THAT YOU HAVE A DIFFERENT VALUE SYSTEM. SARTRE TELLS US...

COOL IT, "FOUR EYES"! GIMME YOUR CASH, LADY!
HOWARD DOESN'T GIVE ME MY ALLOWANCE TILL TOMORROW.

HOW ABOUT CREDIT CARDS?
SURE! HERE'S ONE FOR THE DRY CLEANERS, HERE'S ONE FOR THE MILKMAN...

THIS IS SUPPOSED TO BE THE AFFLUENT SUBURBS!
WE'VE SPENT SO MUCH BEING AFFLUENT, WE DON'T HAVE ANY EXPENSIVE STUFF.
OK, I'M GOING, BUT I'M TAKING THE PLASTIC FLAMINGOES!
WIPE YOUR FEET ON THE WAY OUT!

YOU'VE HIT ON THE ULTIMATE BURGLAR SNARE - LIVING BEYOND YOUR MEANS.

"WOODS," I GOT YOU A DYNAMITE GIG! RIGHT UP YOUR ALLEY: YOU AND A PRIEST ON CHRISTIANITY AND JUDAISM.
THEY WANNA ESTABLISH AN INTER-FAITH DIALOGUE.
BUT I'M NO EXPERT ON JUDAISM.
THAT'S THE BEAUTY PART, YOU DON'T HAVE TO BE. THEY WANT YOU TO TAKE A DIVE.

Sale
Foot-Stools
HAND MIRRORS
SUITCASES
THIS STORE IS TOO LITERAL.
IF YOU WANT TO COMPLAIN, THE MANAGER IS IN THERE.
HEAD OFFICE

AHH...IT'S NOT CROWDED...

HERE'S A NICE SPOT...

"I WAS LYING ON A BEACH WHEN A BULLY THREW SAND IN MY FACE
HERE'S SAND IN YOUR EYE... HA! HA!
I DON'T MIND IT... ANYBODY CAN THROW SAND IN MY FACE AS LONG AS THEY'RE SINCERE.

"BUT WHEN THE SAME BULLY CAME BY FOR 3 STRAIGHT DAYS AND THREW SAND IN MY FACE...

"-I DECIDED TO DO SOMETHING ABOUT IT, BECAUSE IT WAS GETTING RIDICULOUS. SO I TOOK DANCING LESSONS.
Learn to DANCE
TANGO SALSA MAMBO
1 FLITE UP
WA

"TRUE, THAT WOULDN'T HELP ME DEFEND MYSELF, BUT AT LEAST I COULD PROVIDE A MOVING TARGET.
"2 WEEKS LATER, I'M LYING ON THE BEACH, AND AS HE'S ABOUT TO THROW SAND IN MY FACE...

"I BREAK OUT INTO A TANGO.
IT TOOK HIM SO COMPLETELY OFF GUARD, HE DROPPED HIS SAND AND STARTED TO TANGO ALONG WITH ME, BUT...
"WHILE I WAS TRYING TO FIGURE OUT MY NEXT MOVE, WE WERE BOTH ARRESTED BY THE VICE SQUAD FOR DANCING IN A PUBLIC PLACE WITHOUT GIRLS"
POLIC

YOU ACADEMICS! YOU'LL PUBLISH ANYTHING, JUST SO YOU CAN SAY YOU'VE PUBLISHED.
THAT'S A BIT HARSH.
IT IS? LOOK HOW THIS BOOK IS PADDED!
400 PAGES, AND TWO ENTRIES IN THE INDEX: Contents pp 1-400.
More Contents, see Volumes II-VI.

MARTIANS ARE SPYING ON ME!!
THEY FOLLOW ME EVERYWHERE! TAP MY PHONE! SHOOT RADIO-ACTIVE RAYS AT ME IN MY HOUSE!
I FEEL THE SAME WAY, BUT I DRESS BETTER...